CONTENTS

D1431221

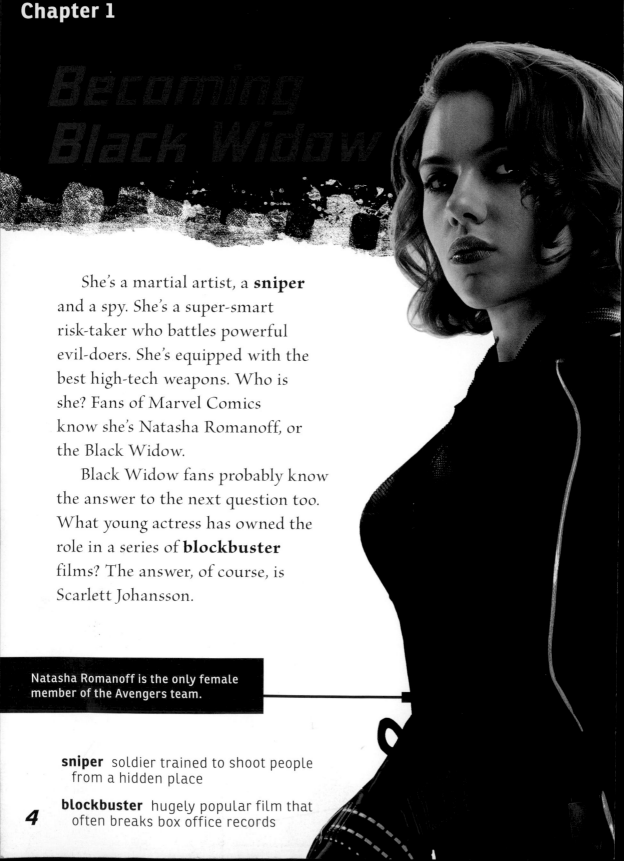

Chapter 1

Becoming Black Widow

She's a martial artist, a **sniper** and a spy. She's a super-smart risk-taker who battles powerful evil-doers. She's equipped with the best high-tech weapons. Who is she? Fans of Marvel Comics know she's Natasha Romanoff, or the Black Widow.

Black Widow fans probably know the answer to the next question too. What young actress has owned the role in a series of **blockbuster** films? The answer, of course, is Scarlett Johansson.

Natasha Romanoff is the only female member of the Avengers team.

sniper soldier trained to shoot people from a hidden place

blockbuster hugely popular film that often breaks box office records

Scarlett first showed up as Black Widow in 2010's *Iron Man 2*. Black Widow then played a major role in 2012's smash hit *Marvel Avengers Assemble*. Her next appearance as Black Widow was in *Captain America: The Winter Soldier* (2014). Two more appearances quickly followed, in *Avengers: Age of Ultron* (2015), and *Captain America: Civil War* (2016). It's likely that Scarlett will appear in more Black Widow adventures in the future.

"She knows what people think of her. She lets you in a little bit and then she closes the door. I think it's exciting to be able to get a peek every now and again ... I like that part of her personality."

– Scarlett on her character Black Widow

Risky business

The success of the Marvel film series has brought Scarlett Johansson fame as an action star. But this talented actress is so much more.

Like her Black Widow character, Scarlett loves taking risks in her work. She has said that doing the same thing repeatedly would "be a waste". She says she "feels more comfortable" playing it risky. Her history as a performer proves these words many times over.

opposite page: Here Scarlett is seen with her grandmother, younger sister, Fenan, and her mother.

Action hero is not Scarlett's only film identity. She's appeared in films of nearly every **genre**. She's lent her voice to characters in animated films. She's acted on the stage and modelled in fashion adverts. She's even written song lyrics and produced two CDs – singing her own songs and those of others. Considering Scarlett's long list of credits, one might wonder if there is anything this talented actress *can't* do.

genre category or style of music, literature or art

It's in the genes

Scarlett's desire to express herself probably comes from her creative family. Her grandfather, Ejner Bainkamp Johansson, was a screenwriter and producer. Her father, Karsten Johansson, is an architect. Her mother, Melanie Sloan, has worked as a film and television producer. Scarlett's older sister, Vanessa, is also an actress.

Chapter 2

An early start

Scarlett Ingrid Johansson seems like she was born to be in the limelight. Her success has come earlier and more easily than for most young hopefuls who give acting a shot.

Scarlett and her twin brother, Hunter, were born on 22 November 1984, in New York City, USA. She came into the world three minutes before he did. At the age of three Scarlett already knew that she wanted to be an actor. Her first paying job came in 1993. She acted in a skit for the TV programme *Late Night with Conan O'Brien*. She was just eight years old.

Scarlett's twin brother, Hunter, has also worked in films but now has a career in politics.

."I've always been a big ham.
It's like I popped out of the womb
and said 'I will perform!'"
– Scarlett on her acting career

Even before Scarlett appeared
on Conan's TV programme, her
mother took her to audition for
TV adverts. But adverts weren't
Scarlett's dream job. She's said
that auditioning for these small
parts was "awful". She found the
other mums "scary", and that the
whole experience was too much
like being in a beauty contest. Not
winning a part always made her
miserable. But it didn't mean she
was ready to give up on acting
altogether.

From stage to screen

Scarlett's next acting experience took her into theatres to perform for live audiences. In October 1993 she began appearing in the off-Broadway play *Sophistry*. She had only a couple of lines, but her repeated performances helped her to gain confidence. She also improved her acting skills by taking weekend lessons.

Her efforts paid off. Scarlett was cast in her first film at just 9 years old. She played the daughter of actor John Ritter in the 1994 comedy *North*.

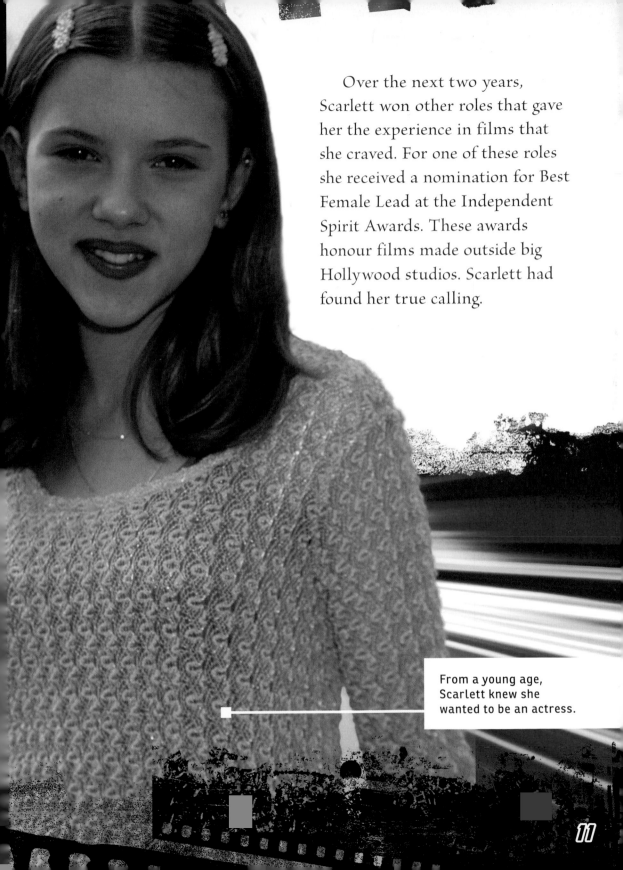

Over the next two years, Scarlett won other roles that gave her the experience in films that she craved. For one of these roles she received a nomination for Best Female Lead at the Independent Spirit Awards. These awards honour films made outside big Hollywood studios. Scarlett had found her true calling.

From a young age, Scarlett knew she wanted to be an actress.

13 going on 30

What causes people to notice actors and turn them into stars? The answers are different for every celebrity. For Scarlett it was her maturity that brought attention early on. She had a quiet intensity. Her voice was husky, even as a young girl. These qualities helped Scarlett stand out as a young actor. They also helped her to land an important film role.

The film was 1998's *The Horse Whisperer*, starring and directed by Robert Redford. Scarlett's onscreen credit read "Introducing Scarlett Johansson". She played Grace, a young girl who finds her way back to happiness after a tragic horse riding accident. It was Scarlett's sixth film role and many praised her work. Robert Redford famously noted that Scarlett was "13 going on 30".

Some film critics said the character of Grace was Scarlett's "break-out role". But Scarlett's true big break was still a few years off.

Scarlett was just 13 years old when she played Grace in *The Horse Whisperer*.

"Unfortunately, because it's adults writing these scripts, it's tough [for young actors to find realistic roles]. The problem is that adults portray kids like mall rats and not seriously ... Kids and teenagers just aren't being portrayed with any real depth."

– Scarlett at 13 on finding good parts

Chapter 3

Earning star status

With her success in *The Horse Whisperer*, Scarlett's star began to climb rapidly. More and better film scripts began coming her way. With her mum acting as her manager, Scarlett took on several more roles in her teenage years. Two stand outs were released in 2003.

The first was *Girl With a Pearl Earring*. Scarlett played Griet, a peasant girl who becomes a model for the famous painter Johannes Vermeer, played by Colin Firth. With few lines and an ability to quietly express many emotions, Scarlett stole hearts. She had the press buzzing. Many again noted her "quiet intensity".

Scarlett was rewarded for her work with eight Best Actress nominations. These included a highly respected Golden Globe nomination from the Hollywood Foreign Press Association. Of these nominations, Scarlett won three.

"Colin kept saying I looked like a peeled egg [or] a Q-Tip [cotton bud]. He'd stick little Q-Tips with happy faces ... on our make-up mirror."

– Scarlett on her white-scarf-wrapped head as Griet

The big breakthrough

Scarlett's second film that came out in 2003 was *Lost in Translation*. It would be the film that turned Scarlett Johansson into a sought-after celebrity.

Lost in Translation was a mature drama. Scarlett played Charlotte, a young woman who befriends an aging, downhearted film star. Scarlett was only 17 when the film was made. But the character she played was in her early 20s. The role marked Scarlett's move into playing adult characters. She received even more Best Actress nominations than she did for *Girl with a Pearl Earring*. She went on to win four out of 22 nominations. The most respected award was from The British Academy of Film and Television Arts (BAFTA).

gross earn or bring in

The film's director, Sofia Coppola, felt Scarlett was "unique" and mature enough to play an older character. Sofia told a reporter, "I like the way she's able to convey feelings without doing much. She's subtle."

The media more than agreed. Scores of reviews expressed high praise for Scarlett's acting. She was on her way to even greater heights of stardom.

Scarlett played Charlotte in *Lost in Translation*. She starred with Bill Murray, who is seen on the opposite page.

"Once you lose your anonymity, you always crave it. You never get it back."

– Scarlett on becoming famous

Smooth moves

In the next few years, Scarlett starred in 16 more films. During this time she managed to move smoothly from child actor to major star. Scarlett chose a wide variety of roles. She appeared in romantic comedies, crime drama and fantasy films. The acclaimed writer-director Woody Allen cast her in three of his films during this time.

Scarlett did most of her own stunts and fight sequences in *Iron Man 2*.

Scarlett (seated on the left) starred with Chris Evans (at the bottom of this picture) in *The Perfect Score*.

Scarlett first worked with Chris Evans in the 2004 comedy *The Perfect Score*, in which she played a high school student. Scarlett and Chris later met again to play Black Widow and Captain America.

In 2006, Scarlett appeared in *The Prestige*, a drama involving magicians. In 2008 she appeared in the historical drama *The Other Boleyn Girl*. Scarlett played Mary, the sister of Anne Boleyn, who was married to King Henry VIII.

By this time, Scarlett had already started feeling the thrill of appearing in action films. In 2005 she played a human clone on the run from the government in *The Island*. In 2008 she starred as Silken Floss, the sidekick of the evil Octopus in *The Spirit*. Scarlett then made her first appearance as Black Widow in *Iron Man 2* (2010). By then, no one could deny she had become a major worldwide celebrity.

19

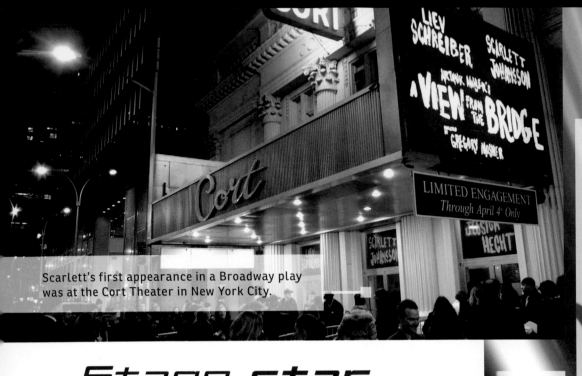

Scarlett's first appearance in a Broadway play was at the Cort Theater in New York City.

Stage star

Scarlett set other goals for herself outside of films. She had always loved the theatre, and in 2010 another dream came true for her. She appeared for the first time on Broadway, the centre of New York's theatre world. She starred in a **revival** of the 1950s play *A View From the Bridge*. Scarlett earned a Tony Award for Best Performance by a Featured Actress in a Play. The Tony Awards are the theatre community's most respected prizes. She appeared on Broadway again in 2013 in the play *Cat on a Hot Tin Roof*.

revival bringing back something that started and existed in the past

Making music

Earlier in her career, Scarlett tried her hand at making music. In 2006 she sang "Summertime" on a compilation CD. Two years later, she released an album called *Anywhere I lay My Head*. Almost every song she sang on the CD was by Tom Waits, a favourite singer-songwriter. She later released another album, *Break Up*, and several singles. But acting in films is the main thing on Scarlett's mind.

"Being welcomed into this community has been an absolute dream come true for me. Ever since I was a little girl, I wanted to be on Broadway and here I am. Unbelievable."

– Scarlett on accepting her Tony Award

Scarlett received glowing reviews for her performance in *A View from the Bridge*.

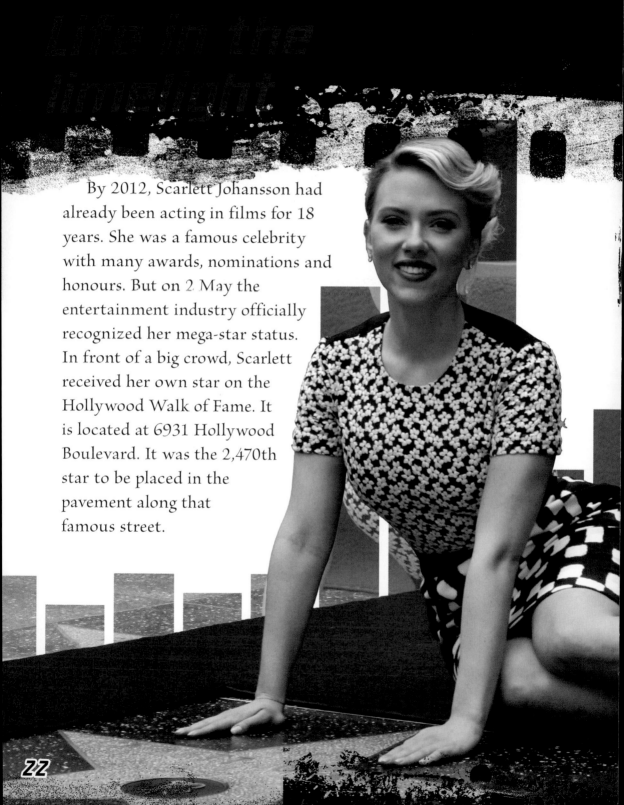

By 2012, Scarlett Johansson had
already been acting in films for 18
years. She was a famous celebrity
with many awards, nominations and
honours. But on 2 May the
entertainment industry officially
recognized her mega-star status.
In front of a big crowd, Scarlett
received her own star on the
Hollywood Walk of Fame. It
is located at 6931 Hollywood
Boulevard. It was the 2,470th
star to be placed in the
pavement along that
famous street.

A nickname for Scarlett

Once the media started focusing on Scarlett, it wasn't about to stop. She had talent, beauty and mass public appeal. The one thing she didn't have was a nickname. Scarlett Johansson was a pretty long name to keep repeating in news stories. So someone began referring to her as "ScarJo". The unfortunate nickname stuck, and it's become widespread in the media. But Scarlett hates it! "I associate it with, like, pop stars," she says. "It sounds tacky. It's lazy and flippant ... and there's something kind of violent [and] insulting about it."

Two days later *The Avengers* opened in cinemas across the United States. (The film was called *Marvel Avengers Assemble* in the UK.) The film was a worldwide smash hit. Again playing Black Widow, Scarlett was the stand-out woman among a pack of male superheroes. These included Iron Man (Robert Downey, Jr), Captain America (Chris Evans), the Hulk (Mark Ruffalo), Thor (Chris Hemsworth) and Hawkeye (Jeremy Renner).

Unlike *Iron Man 2*, in *Marvel Avengers Assemble* Natasha Romanoff was given a lot more screen time. This raised Scarlett's visibility and appeal as an action film star in a major way.

Black Widow reprised

In 2014 Scarlett got the chance to **reprise** her role as Black Widow yet again. Natasha Romanoff appeared in the film *Captain America: The Winter Soldier*. This time the two heroes teamed up to bring down a dangerous killer known as the Winter Soldier.

This film was different from the earlier Marvel films. Unlike the others, *Winter Soldier* used real live action scenes rather than computer graphics. That meant the characters worked especially hard to make their fight scenes look realistic. Scarlett trained for these moments with fierce dedication. She is proud of the fact that she performed the majority of the stunts herself. Only the most dangerous ones were performed by her stunt double.

reprise repeat a performance of a role

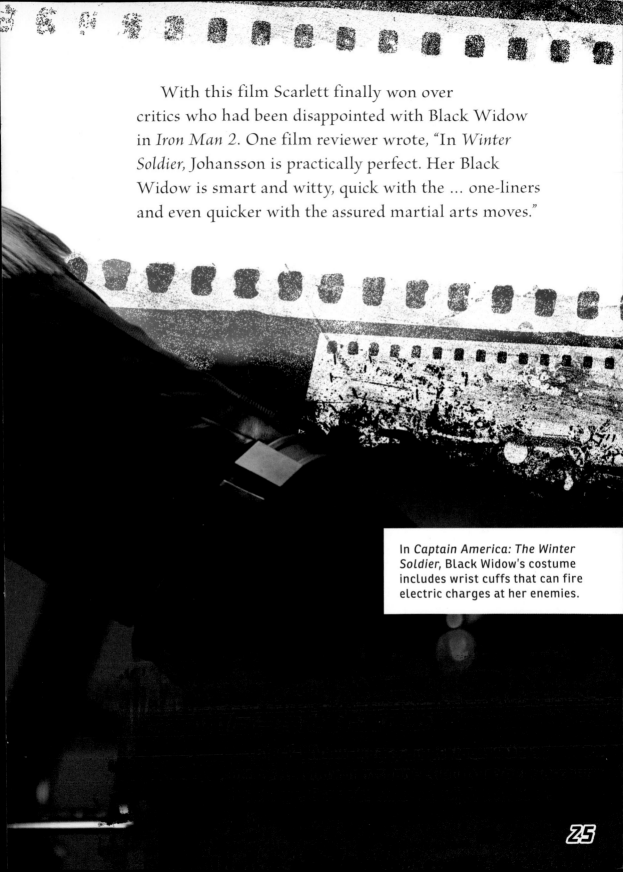

With this film Scarlett finally won over critics who had been disappointed with Black Widow in *Iron Man 2*. One film reviewer wrote, "In *Winter Soldier*, Johansson is practically perfect. Her Black Widow is smart and witty, quick with the ... one-liners and even quicker with the assured martial arts moves."

In *Captain America: The Winter Soldier*, Black Widow's costume includes wrist cuffs that can fire electric charges at her enemies.

Winter Soldier received multiple award nominations. This time Scarlett received five, including Favorite Female Action Star at the Kids' Choice awards.

Next up for her in the action genre was *Avengers: Age of Ultron* in 2015. Natasha Romanoff didn't see much action in *Age of Ultron*. However, Scarlett was nominated for Sci-fi/Fantasy Choice Movie Actress at the Teen Choice Awards.

Since *Age of Ultron*, Scarlett has been busier than ever, working in all kinds of films. In 2016 she appeared in three very different films. In *Hail, Caesar!* she played an actress in 1950s Hollywood. In *The Jungle Book*, she voiced the python character Kaa. And she returned to the role of Natasha Romanoff in *Captain America: Civil War*.

"I would never knowingly go into a film that I wouldn't pay to see, or something that didn't challenge me."

– Scarlett on choosing film roles

27

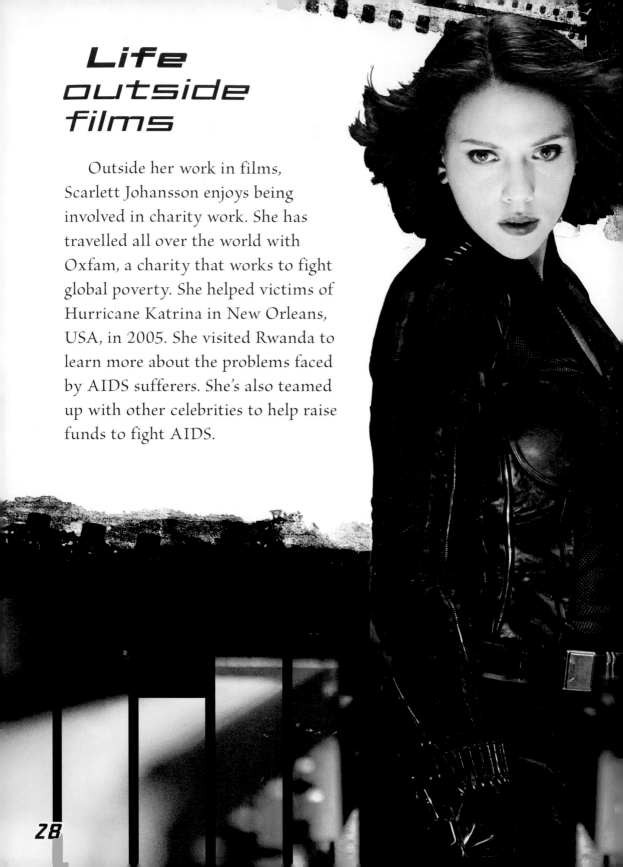

Life outside films

Outside her work in films, Scarlett Johansson enjoys being involved in charity work. She has travelled all over the world with Oxfam, a charity that works to fight global poverty. She helped victims of Hurricane Katrina in New Orleans, USA, in 2005. She visited Rwanda to learn more about the problems faced by AIDS sufferers. She's also teamed up with other celebrities to help raise funds to fight AIDS.

Another shot at the action

Scarlett fans will see more of her in the next few years. She has plenty more films in the pipeline, including action films.

Scarlett has proven herself up to pretty much any challenge she's faced as an actor. Whether as an action star or a dramatic scene-stealer, she's bound to keep surprising her fans. It's safe to say Scarlett Johansson has arrived.

GLOSSARY

blockbuster hugely popular film that often breaks box office records

genre category or style of music, literature or art

gross earn or bring in

reprise repeat a performance of a role

revival bringing back something that started and existed in the past

sniper soldier trained to shoot people from a hidden place

FIND OUT MORE

BOOKS

Black Widow: This is Black Widow (World of Reading), Clarissa S. Wong (Marvel Press, 2015)

How to Make a Movie in 10 Easy Lessons (Super Skills), Robert Blofield (QED, 2015)

Marvel Avengers: The Ultimate Character Guide, Alan Cowsill (DK Children, 2015)

Scarlett Johansson: Hollywood Superstar (People to Know Today), Michael Schuman (Enslow Publishers, 2011)

WEBSITES

www.dogomovies.com/category/action
Read children's reviews of action films.

**kids.britannica.com/comptons/article-9610085/
Scarlett-Johansson**
Find out more about Scarlett's life.

marvelkids.disney.co.uk/avengers
Learn more about the Avengers and try out some games and activities.

INDEX